MORE OPPOSITES

Also by Richard Wilbur:

MORE
OPPOSITES

written and illustrated by
RICHARD WILBUR

HBJ

HARCOURT BRACE JOVANOVICH, PUBLISHERS

New York   San Diego   London

Requests for permission to make copies of
any part of the work should be mailed to:
Permissions Department,
Harcourt Brace Jovanovich, Publishers, 8th Floor,
Orlando, Florida 32887.

Library of Congress Cataloging-in-Publication Data
Wilbur, Richard, 1921–
More Opposites/written and illustrated
by Richard Wilbur.
p.   cm.
Summary: A collection of humorous poems
centering around words and their opposites.
ISBN 0-15-170072-9
1. English language — Synonyms and antonyms — Poetry.
2. Humorous poetry, American. [1. English
language — Synonyms and antonyms — Poetry.
2. American poetry. 3. Humorous poetry.]   I. Title.
PS3545.I32165M67   1991
811'.52 — dc20   91-14411

Printed in Mexico
First edition
A B C D E

Poems #4, #8, #9, #15, #16, #18, #24, and #28
first appeared in *Cricket* magazine in 1990.
Poems #5, #17, #19, and #23 first appeared in *The
Formalist* in 1990.

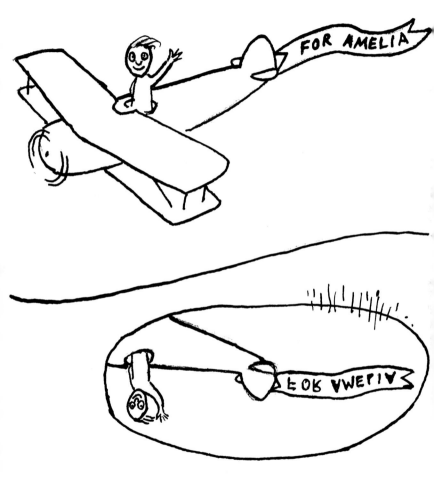

1

The opposite of *duck* is *drake*.
Remember that, for heaven's sake!
One's female, and the other's male.
In writing to a *drake*, don't fail
To start your letter off, "Dear Sir."
"Dear Madam" is what *ducks* prefer.

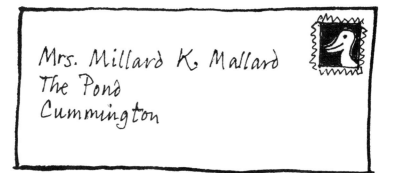

In snowball fights, the opposite
Of *duck*, of course, is *getting hit*.

2

The opposite of *doctor*? Well,
That's not so very hard to tell.
A *doctor*'s nice, and when you're ill
He makes you better with a pill.
Then what's his opposite? Don't be thick!
It's *anyone who makes you sick.*

3

What is the opposite of *baby*?
The answer is a *grown-up*, maybe.

4

What is the opposite of *pillow*?
The answer, child, is *armadillo*.
"Oh, don't talk nonsense!" you protest.
However, if you tried to rest
Your head upon the creature, you
Would find that what I say is true.
It isn't soft. From head to tail
It wears a scratchy coat of mail.
And furthermore, it won't hold still
Upon a bed, as pillows will,
But squirms, and jumps at every chance
To run away and eat some ants.

So there! Admit that I was right,
Or else we'll have a *pillow fight*.

5

The opposite of *tar* is *rat*.
If you don't see the sense of that,
Just spell *tar* backwards, and you will.
And there's another reason still:
Though *rats* desert a sinking ship,
A *tar*, with stiffened upper lip,
Will man the bilge-pumps like a sport
And bring the vessel into port.

6

The opposite of *sheep*, I think,
Is when you cannot sleep a wink
And find that you're not counting rams
And ewes and little jumping lambs
But countless *vultures* flocking by
With bony head and searching eye,
Each giving you a sidewise glare
To let you know it knows you're there.

7

How often travelers who mean
To tell us of some cave they've seen
Fall mute, forgetting how to use
Two dreadful words which they confuse!
The word *stalactite* is the first;
Stalagmite means the same, reversed.
Though both these things are formed in time
By dripping carbonate of lime,
Stalactites *hang*, while from beneath,
Stalagmites *rise* like lower teeth.

Can you remember that? You'll find
That you can fix those facts in mind
If you will frequently repeat,
While strolling down the village street
Or waiting for a bus to town,
"Stalagmites up! Stalactites down!"

Take care, though, not to be too loud,
Or you may draw a curious crowd.

8

An *omen* is a sign of some
Occurrence that is *yet to come*,
As when a star, by tumbling down,
Warns that a king will lose his crown.

A *clue*, by contrast, is a sign
By means of which we can divine
What has already taken place —
As when, to cite a common case,
A fish is missing from a platter,
And the cat looks a little fatter.

9

What is the opposite of *road*?
I'd say the answer is *abode*.
"What's an abode?" you ask. I'd say
It's ground that doesn't lead away—
Some patch of earth where you *abide*
Because it makes you satisfied.

Abodes don't take you anywhere,
Because you are already there.

10

The opposite of *"Gee!"* is some
Reaction that is bored and glum,
Like *saying "Big deal" with a shrug,*
Or *staring mutely at the rug.*

When *"Gee!"* is spoken to a horse,
It bids him take a right-hand course.
Conversely, *"Haw!"* is how to say
"Turn left" and make a horse obey.

"But will a SEA-horse," you inquire,
"Turn *gee* or *haw* as you desire,
Or must you speak of *starboard* and
Of *port* to make him understand?"

How foolish such a question is!
Don't interrupt me, please. *Gee whiz!*

11

The opposite of *kite*, I'd say,
Is *yo-yo*. On a breezy day
You take your *kite* and let it *rise*
Upon its string into the skies,
And then you pull it *down* with ease
(Unless it crashes in the trees).
A *yo-yo*, though, drops *down*, and then
You quickly bring it *up* again
By pulling deftly on its string
(If you can work the blasted thing).

12

When ships send out an *S.O.S.*
It means that they are in distress.
Is there an opposite sort of call
Which means "There's nothing wrong at all"?
Of course not. Ships would think it sappy
To send us word that they are happy.
If you hear *nothing* from a liner,
It means that things could not be finer.

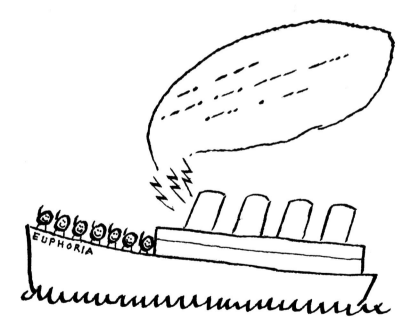

13

When some poor thirsty nomad sees
A far-off fountain fringed with trees
And, making for the spot in haste
Across the blazing desert waste,
Finds that his vision had no basis,
That is the opposite of *oasis*.
What do we call such sad confusion?
Mirage, or *optical illusion*.

Another opposite might be
A sandy islet in the sea.

14

The opposite of *robber*? Come,
You know the answer. Don't be dumb!
While robbers *take things* for a living,
Philanthropists are fond of *giving*.
"And yet," you say, "that's not quite true;
Philanthropists are takers, too,
And often have been very greedy
Before they thought to help the needy."

Well, let's be obvious, then: the op-
Posite of *robber* is a *cop*.

15

The opposite of *less* is *more*.
What's better? Which one are you for?
My question may seem simple, but
The catch is — more or less of *what*?

"Let's have more everything!" you cry.
Well, after we have had more pie,
More pickles, and more layer cake,
I think we'll want *less stomach-ache*.

The best thing's to avoid excess.
Try to be temperate, more or less.

16

An *echo*'s opposite is the *cry*
To which the echo makes reply.
Of course I do not mean to claim
That what they say is not the same.
If one of them calls out "Good day"
Or "Who are you?" or "Hip, hooray"
Or "Robert has an ugly hat,"
The other says exactly that.
But still they're opposites. Know why?
A cry is *bold*; an echo's *shy*,
And though it loves to shout yoo-hoo,
It won't until it hears from you.

17

What is the opposite of *root*?
It's *stem and branch and leaf and fruit* —
All of a plant that we can see.
Another answer, possibly,
Is *when a truffle-hunter's pig
Has grown too proud to sniff and dig,
And stands there with his snout in air*.
(Such happenings are very rare.)

18

A *dragon* is a wingèd snake
Who's always fierce and wide awake
And squats in front of caves which hold
Enormous bags and chests of gold.
If you approach, he bares his nails
And roars at you, and then exhales
Fire, smoke, and sulphur — all of which
Dissuade you from becoming rich.

A dragon's opposite is a *goose*,
A bird who likes to be of use
And who (if of a special breed)
Will give you all you really need
By laying for you every day
A golden egg (or so they say).

19

The opposite of *stunt*? You're right!
It's *making someone grow in height*
By feeding him nutritious bran
Till he's a large and smiling man.
Another answer is *when you*
Do something not too hard to do,
Some act that doesn't call for nerve
And isn't thrilling to observe,
Like sipping from a water glass
Or merely lying on the grass.

20

The opposite of *so-and-so*
Is *anyone whose name you know,*

Or *someone good* who would not take
Your skateboard or your piece of cake,
Making you tell him, with a thwack,
"You so-and-so! I want that back!"

21

The opposite of *punch*, I think,
Might be some sort of *fruitless drink*,
Unless we say that *punch* means *hit*,
In which event the opposite
Is *counter-punch* or *shadow-box*.
Or if we think of *punching clocks*,
I guess the opposite of *punch*
Is *always to be out to lunch*.

What if we capitalize the P?
Judy's the answer then, since she
And *Punch*, although they chose to marry,
Are each the other's adversary —
Each having, ever since they wed,
Pounded the other on the head.

How many things we've thought of! Whew!
I'm getting punchy. That will do.

22

A *spell* is something you are under
When put to sleep, or filled with wonder.
The opposite of *spell*, I guess,
Is *normal waking consciousness*,
In which you're not enthralled or sleepy,
And things are only *fairly* creepy.

Another answer could be *writing*
"*Recieve*," "*Occassional*," and "*fiteing*,"
"*Emporer*," "*mackeral*," and "*snaiks*,"
And other horribel mistaiks.

23

The opposite of *hot*, we know,
Is *icy cold* or *ten below*.
Some other answers to the question
Are *leaky buckets*, *indigestion*,
E-minus, or a *granny knot*,
Since all those things are *not so hot*.

24

The opposite of *moth*? It's *moth*!
One kind is fond of chewing cloth
And biting holes in woolen hats
And coats and dresses and cravats.

However, it's another story
With a nice moth called *Bombyx Mori*,
Who, when it is of tender age
And passing through the larval stage,
Sits munching in a mulberry tree
And spinning silk for you and me —
Of which we make, of course, cravats
As well as dresses, coats, and hats.

25

The opposite of *top*, in case
You haven't heard, is *bottom*, *base*,
Foundation, *underside*, or *foot*.
I also think of *chimney soot*
And *mattresses* and *margarine*,
Since none of those is fun to spin.

When you are playing on a harp,
The opposite of *flat* is *sharp*,
And both sound very good if they
Are what the music says to play.
But when you think it's time to stop
And drink a bit of soda pop,
How bad the thought of flatness is!
A soda should be *full of fizz*.

27

Gray is the opposite of *blue*,
Or was in 1862.

At present, *blue* means *sad and tearful*,
And so its opposite is *cheerful*.

28

What is the opposite of *chew*?
It's *wolf*, which you must never do.
A wolf is said to *wolf* his food,
Because he gulps it down unchewed.
If you must imitate a beast,
Then let it be the cow, at least,
Who eats in such a placid way
And never hurries through her hay.

The cow, however, has a trait
Which there's no need to imitate.
Don't go too far! Don't overdo it!
Chew what you eat, but don't *re*-chew it.
I fear you'd be a social dud
If you were seen to have a *cud*.

29

What is the opposite of a *U*?
An *arch* to knock croquet balls through,
Using a mallet which could be
Described as an inverted *T*.

But how can you invert an *O*?
It's round on top and round below.
It looks as though a croquet ball
May have no opposite at all.

30

I wonder if you've ever seen a
Willow sheltering a *hyena*?
Nowhere in nature can be found
An opposition more profound:
A sad tree weeping inconsolably!
A wild beast laughing uncontrollably!

31

The opposite of *pluck*, my dear,
Is *being overcome by fear*.
(I've thought of one more opposite,
But I don't think I'll mention it,
Since, frankly, I have never heard
Of *adding feathers to a bird*.)

32

The opposite of *sound*? Well, that's
When someone's *ill*, or *wrong*, or *bats*,
Or when some firm is *deep in debt*.
Another answer's *what you get*
By strumming cobwebs with a feather
Or banging powder puffs together.

33

What is the opposite of *Missouri*?
The answer's *California*, surely.
Missouri folk are *doubters* who
Won't take your word for two plus two
Until they add them up, by heck,
And then they like to double-check.

But people on our Western Coast
Believe in everything, almost.
The Californians think, I'm told,
That every river's full of gold,

That stars give good advice to men
On what they ought to do, and when,
And that we all had former lives
As Pharaohs or as Pharaohs' wives.

That's how those states are opposite.
I may exaggerate a bit,
But I have told you what we say
In *Massachusetts*, anyway.

34

The opposite of *stop* is *go*,
But sometimes one does both, you know.
We've come at last, by pleasant stages,
To where there are no further pages,
And since our book is at an end,
I'll *stop*. And *go*. Farewell, my friend.